# Sit

Written by Caroline Green
Illustrated by Adriana Predoi

**Collins**

# sip

# tap

sip

tap

# sit

. . .

# tip

7

sit

tip

# nap

10

pat

. . .

nap

pat

/s/

14

#  Review: After reading

Use your assessment from hearing the children read to choose any GPCs and words that need additional practice.

## Read 1: Decoding

- Use grapheme cards to make any words you need to practise. Model reading those words, using teacher-led blending.
- Look at the "I spy sounds" pages (14–15) together. Ask the children to point out as many things as they can in the picture that begin with the /s/ sound. (*sun, scooter, slippers, stars, sailing boat, sunglasses, snow, snowman, string, scissors, spoon, skates, spider, stairs, sink*)
- Ask the children to follow as you read the whole book, demonstrating fluency and prosody.

## Read 2: Vocabulary

- Look back through the book and discuss the pictures. Encourage the children to talk about details that stand out for them. Use a dialogic talk model to expand on their ideas and recast them in full sentences as naturally as possible.
- Work together to expand vocabulary by naming objects in the pictures that children do not know.
- Reread pages 2 and 11. For each, encourage the children to mime the words **sip** and **pat**, to check their understanding.

## Read 3: Comprehension

- Turn to pages 6 and 7. Talk about any times the children have seen something tip over. Ask: What tipped? What happened next?
- Talk about the story, drawing on any knowledge the children already have about Goldilocks and the Three Bears. For example, on pages 2 and 3, ask: Who do you think lives in this house? Why? (e.g. *three bears; there are three chairs and there are pictures of bears on the wall*) On pages 10 and 11, ask: Whose bed is Goldilocks in? How do you know? (e.g. *the baby bear's; it is the smallest bed*)